Life's Instructions for
WISDOM, SUCCESS,
AND HAPPINESS

Life's Instructions for
WISDOM, SUCCESS,
AND HAPPINESS

H. Jackson Brown, Jr.

RUTLEDGE HILL PRESS
NASHVILLE, TENNESSEE
A Division of Thomas Nelson Publishers
Since 1798

www.thomasnelson.com

Published by Rutledge Hill Press, a Division of Thomas Nelson, Inc.,
P.O. Box 141000, Nashville, Tennessee 37214.

Rutledge Hill Press books may be purchased in bulk for educational,
business, fundraising, or sales promotional use. For information,
please e-mail SpecialMarkets@ThomasNelson.com.

Library of Congress Cataloging-in-Publication Data

Life's instructions for wisdom, success, and happiness / [compiled by] H. Jackson
Brown, Jr.
  p. cm.
  ISBN 1-4016-0235-5
  1. Conduct of life—Quotations, maxims, etc. 2. Success—Quotations,
maxims, etc. 3. Happiness—Quotations, maxims, etc. I. Brown, H. Jackson, 1940–
PN6084.C556 L54 2000
082—dc21

00-046008

Printed in the United States of America

05 06 07 08 09 — 5 4 3 2 1

For more information regarding Mr. Brown's books, please visit his Web site at

www.instructionbook.com

or write to him at

H. Jackson Brown, Jr.
P.O. Box 150155
Nashville, TN 37215

Contents

Introduction

THE THREE SUBJECTS of this book, wisdom, success, and happiness, are universally pursued and what we all wish for ourselves and for the ones we love.

Of the three, wisdom can be the most illusive. I've read that you can inherit wealth but never wisdom. For most of us wisdom is acquired in the thicket of experience and usually meets us somewhere along the way if we live long enough. But sooner is better than later. Like the Iowa farmer observed, the trick is to get wise before you get old.

Our success is often determined by how well we balance the demands of family, career, faith, and community. The words of Bessie Anderson Stanley might help us keep things in perspective: "he has achieved success who has lived well, laughed often, and loved much." My father had his own idea, "Judge your success," he advised, "by measuring how far you've come with the talents you've been given." His words and his life were a reminder that a successful life doesn't require that we've done *the* best, but that we've done *our* best. The world whirls and the planets spin, but the chiseled words remain—self-discipline, integrity, kindness, honesty, and courage are still the essentials to successful living.

My own happiness, I've discovered, can be greatly enhanced by greeting each day with an attitude of gratitude and by appreciating and finding delight in life's simple pleasures. This observation from Thorton Wilder in *Our Town* has always been one of my favorites, "...clocks ticking...and Momma's sunflowers, and food, and coffee, and new-ironed dresses, and hot baths... and sleeping, and waking up. Oh, earth, you're too wonderful for anybody to realize you." This is a gentle reminder that happiness is most often found not over the horizon or around the bend, but in small things and simple moments back home on the front porch.

—H. JACKSON BROWN, JR.
Tall Pine Lodge
Fernvale, Tennessee

WISDOM

1. Remember that knowledge is powerless unless acted upon.

2. Pay less attention to what people say and more attention to what they do.

3. Remember that doing anything well is going to take longer than you think.

4. Say something every day that encourages your children.

5.   If you know you're going to lose, do it with style.

6.   Remember that all important truths are simple.

7.   Try not to worry about things over which you have no control.

8.   Ask yourself if what you're doing today is getting you closer to where you want to be tomorrow.

Never mistake
knowledge for wisdom.
One helps you
make a living;
the other helps you
make a life.

—SANDRA CAREY

9. Remember that life's big changes rarely give advance warning.

10. Never hesitate to do what you know is right.

11. Question your prejudices.

12. Teach by example.

13. When reading self-help books, include the Bible.

14. Remember the best way to improve your kids is to improve your marriage.

15. Do something every day that maintains your good health.

16. Remember that true wealth is not having all the money you want, but having all the money you need.

Live your life each day
as you would climb a
mountain. An occasional
glance toward the summit
keeps the goal in mind, but
many beautiful scenes are
to be observed from each
new vantage point. Climb
slowly, steadily, enjoying
each passing moment; the
view from the summit will
serve as a fitting climax
for the journey.

—HAROLD V. MERLCHERT

17. Look for something positive in each person you deal with; focus on that attribute when dealing with them.

18. Be faithful.

19. Never claim a victory prematurely.

20. Remember that everything you cherish in life demands from you an obligation.

21. Never forget the debt you owe to all those who have gone before you.

22. Stand up for your principles even if you have to stand alone.

23. Remember that a gesture of friendship, no matter how small, is always appreciated.

You can tell whether a man is clever by his answers. You can tell whether a man is wise by his questions.

—Naguib Mahfouz

24. Offer hope.

25. Remember that life's most treasured moments often come unannounced.

26. Seek respect rather than popularity.

27. Remember that without good character, knowledge and talent are wasted.

28. Never underestimate the things a motivated and determined person can accomplish.

29. Commit yourself to a mighty purpose.

30. Remember that every age brings new opportunities.

31. Remember that you can miss a lot of good things in life by having the wrong attitude.

The price
of wisdom
is beyond
rubies.

—JOB 28:18

32. Teach your children the pride and satisfaction that comes from doing any job well.

33. Ask for advice when you need it, but remember that no one is an expert on your life.

34. Remember that the only dumb question is the one you wanted to ask but didn't.

35.   Make your money before spending it.

36.   Never intentionally embarrass anyone.

37.   Remember that creating a successful marriage is like farming: you have to start over again every morning.

38.   Own a copy of the best movie, the best record album, and the Pulitzer prize-winning novel from the year you were born.

Wisdom
is to see the miracles in the common.

—Ralph Waldo Emerson

39.   Forget your troubles by helping
      others forget theirs.

40.   Remember that the benefits of a life
      lived with enthusiasm and gratitude
      is always available to you.

41.   Don't be too quick to criticize.
      Remember that everyone has
      bad days.

42.   Seek refinement rather than fashion and quality rather than price.

43.   Never marry someone in hope that they'll change later.

44.   Remember that your marriage is like a garden, it always needs tending.

45.   See any detour as an opportunity to experience new things.

Be careful to
*get out of an experience
only the wisdom that is in
it—and stop there; lest we
be like the cat that sits
down on a hot stove lid.
She will never sit down on
a hot stove lid again—and
that is well; but also she
will never sit down on a
cold one anymore.*

—MARK TWAIN

46. When you've made a mistake, ask yourself what you have learned from it.

47. Remember that just a few words of praise or encouragement can make someone's day.

48. Ask an older person you respect to tell you his or her greatest regret.

49. Remember, sometimes it's best just to grin and bear it.

50. Never put in writing something that you wouldn't want someone to read.

51. Be as polite to the custodian as you are to the chairman of the board.

52. When you need to apologize, do it in person.

Nine-tenths
of wisdom
is being wise
in time.

—THEODORE ROOSEVELT

53. Remember that regardless of where you are, not much good happens after midnight.

54. Spend twice as much time praising as you do criticizing.

55. Remember that a successful tomorrow begins today.

56. When you're angry, take a thirty-minute walk; when you're really angry, chop some firewood.

57. Don't forget that we are ultimately judged by what we give, not by what we get.

58. Remember that you are always wrong when you are speaking at the top of your voice.

59. Let your children observe your being generous to those in need.

60. Never be rude to someone who disappears behind a partition to prepare or deliver your food.

Try measuring
*your wealth by what you
are rather than by what
you have. Put the tape
measure around your
heart rather than around
your bank account.*

—ANONYMOUS

61. Remember that most of the time it's not what you say, it's how you say it.

62. Never do business with a man who cheats on his wife.

63. When a child wants to tell you something, look them in the eyes and give them your full attention.

64. Never apologize for your opinion.

65. Remember that big problems are often little problems that were ignored.

66. Never confuse your right to do something with the right thing to do.

67. Say "no" when necessary but say "yes" as often as possible.

I hope I shall
always possess firmness
and virtue enough to
maintain what I consider
to be the most enviable of
all titles: the character
of an "Honest Man."

—GEORGE WASHINGTON

68. Take good care of the child's heart inside of you.

69. Never regret any money spent on fresh flowers or books.

70. Remember that children, marriage, and flower gardens reflect the kind of care they get.

71. Live your life so that someone's always speaking well of you.

72. Believe in your children and tell them often that you do.

73. Associate with the kind of people you aspire to be.

74. Remember that every day we have the power to bless someone's life by word if not by deed.

Do *not consider*
anything for your
interest which makes you
break your word, quiet
your modesty, or incline
you to any practice which
will not bear the light
or look the world
in the face.

—MARCUS AURELIUS

75. When apologizing, never ruin it with an excuse.

76. Bless every day with a generous act.

77. Remember there's still no substitute for individual effort.

78. Make your friends feel that there's something extra special about them.

79. Remember that no relationship is a total waste of time. You can always learn something about yourself.

80. Be an example of what you want to see more of in the world.

81. When hiring, consider character as much as experience.

Whaт is the use
of living if it not be
to strive for noble causes
and to make this muddled
world a better place for
those who will live in it
after we are gone?

—WINSTON CHURCHILL

82. Measure your wealth by what you'd have left if you lost all your money.

83. Enhance every activity with good manners.

84. Remember it's preferable to be in a bad deal with good people than in a good deal with bad people.

85. Learn to be comfortable with problems; that's where personal growth and opportunities lie.

86. Remember things usually look better after a good night's sleep.

87. Hire the best when it comes to lawyers, accountants, and plumbers.

The young men
know the rules.
The old men know
the exceptions.

—OLIVER WENDELL HOLMES

88. Give serendipity a chance. Be flexible and let some things "just happen."

89. Remember it's your example which most influences others.

90. Never speak ill of anyone who's had you as a guest in their home.

91. Remember that happiness and virtue are intrinsically linked.

92. Use your best manners and best silver and china for your family—the ones you love.

93. Remember it's not the high cost of living; it's the cost of high living.

94. When you find yourself in a hurry, be sure you're hurrying to do something that matters.

You must
be the change
you wish to see
in the world.

—GANDHI

95. When visiting a foreign country, be on your best behavior. You are a representative of the United States.

96. Remember that every thing of great value has been paid for by blood, sweat, or tears or all three.

97. Don't mistake cleverness for wisdom.

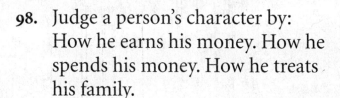

98. Judge a person's character by:
How he earns his money. How he
spends his money. How he treats
his family.

99. When you feel in need of a
compliment, give one to
someone else.

The greatest
use of life is to spend
it for something that
will outlast it.

—WILLIAM JAMES

100. Remember that the biggest challenge we ever face is living up to our own potential.

101. Celebrate victories; analyze defeats.

102. Never forget the three powerful resources you always have available to you; love, prayer, and forgiveness.

103. When you're sad or depressed find something bigger than yourself to think about.

104. Love people more than things.

105. Remember that talent and ability are of little use without integrity.

106. Look for the good. Search for the truth. Hope for the best.

Four things
come not back—
the spoken word, the sped
arrow, the past life,
and the neglected
opportunity.

—ARABIAN PROVERB

107. Remember that everyone you meet is looking for affirmation, direction, and hope.

108. Hold your tongue when you're angry. You'll almost always be glad you did.

109. When deciding matters of great importance, even after you think you have the answer, give it another twenty-four hours.

110. Keep your mind hospitable to
new ideas.

111. Base decisions on what's right not
on who's right.

112. Make your life your sermon.

113. Remember that life's little things
are always more important than
they first appear.

Life is made up,
not of great sacrifices
or duties, but of little
things, in which smiles
and kindness, and small
obligations, given
habitually, are what win
and preserve the heart
and secure comfort.

—SIR HUMPHRY DAVY

114.　If you are going to be an extremist, let it be in the pursuit and protection of your noble values.

115.　Do something daily that helps you grow spiritually.

116.　Stay away from people who belittle your dreams.

117. Learn to say "no" politely and unambiguously.

118. Bad things happen in bad places so stay out of bad places.

119. Never underestimate the peace and confidence that comes from having money in the bank.

Wear a smile
and have friends;
wear a scowl and have
wrinkles. What do we live
for if not to make the
world less difficult
for each other?

—GEORGE ELIOT

120. Keep your word, even to your enemies.

121. Remember that while you can't always be right, you can always be courteous.

122. Never start a business with a person who has more troubles than you.

123. Regardless of the situation, remember that following the Golden Rule will almost always get you through.

124. Don't save your best manners for
people you've just met.

125. Remember that when a woman is
upset, what she usually wants is
understanding not advice.

126. Never keep anything from your
doctor. Some things may be
embarrassing to discuss but it's
nothing he or she hasn't heard
before, and he can't help you if he
doesn't know the whole story.

*Imagination
is more important
than knowledge.
Knowledge is limited.
Imagination encircles
the world.*

—ALBERT EINSTEIN

127.   Remember that when you take inventory of the things you treasure most, none will have been purchased with money.

128.   Welcome change for the opportunity it brings.

129.   Don't criticize people in front of other people. Nobody ever feels better.

130. Never ask "Why me" when bad things happen unless you also ask "Why me" when good things happen.

131. Don't be surprised if your happiest moments are when you are doing things for others.

The purpose of
life is not to be happy.
It is to be useful, to be
honorable, to be
compassionate,
to have it make some
difference that you have
lived and lived well.

—RALPH WALDO EMERSON

132. Remember it's better to trust and be occasionally disappointed than to be distrustful and miserable all the time.

133. Every morning when you wake up, take just 5 seconds and appreciate the fact that in the day that lies before you, all kinds of wonderful things can happen.

134. Remember that the ultimate challenge is not to do something but to be something.

135. Practice preventive maintenance on your car, home, and relationships.

136. Remember that the smallest step towards your goal is worth more than a marathon of intentions.

I *believe*
that every right
implies a responsibility;
every opportunity
an obligation;
every possession
a duty.

—JOHN D. ROCKEFELLER

137.   When considering a new job,
       consider its ability to feed your soul
       as well as your wallet.

138.   Don't waste your time on projects
       and events that are not in harmony
       with your values.

139.   Don't be so casual in dress, language, and manner that people don't take you seriously.

140.   Remember that your life is nothing more than a collection of the choices you have made.

Treasure the
love you receive
above all.
It will survive
long after gold and
good health
have vanished.

—OG MANDINO

141. Make a list of ten guiding principles that you want most to direct your life. Every month or so ask your family or a friend how well you're living up to them.

142. Remember that your attitude as you begin a task often determines how well you finish it.

143. When you want to give yourself a gift, do something nice for someone.

144. Don't leave a foolish mistake until you've come to a wise conclusion.

145. To help your children to become fiscally responsible, let them see you demonstrating good money management.

*Much of wisdom
often goes with
fewest words.*

—SOPHOCLES

146. Remember hard work, honesty, and an enthusiastic approach to life will get you most anything you want.

147. Look on the positive side of things. Life's happiest and most successful people are almost always inspiringly optimistic.

148. When negotiating, never lose your composure. Anger is the worst reason to miss a deal.

❧

149. Even if you're on a strict budget, choose quality over quantity.

❧

150. Remember that debt is always a bad companion.

The art of
being wise is the
art of knowing
what to overlook.

—WILLIAM JAMES

151. When interviewing candidates for a job, ask them their proudest achievements. Then ask them the one mistake they learned from the most.

152. Don't get romantically involved with anyone unless their inner beauty matches their outer beauty.

153. Don't feel you have to express your opinion on every subject.

154. Whatever your present job, even if you're dissatisfied, give it your best shot. This will get you to a better position quicker than anything else you can do.

155. Remember that "no" is one of the most powerful words in your vocabulary. Don't hesitate to use it.

Wisdom does not
show itself so much
in precept as in life—
in a firmness of mind
and mastery of appetite.
It teaches us to do as
well as talk; and to
make our actions
and words all
of a color.

—SENECA

156. Choose your life's mate carefully.
     From this one decision will come
     90 percent of all your happiness
     or misery.

157. Live beneath your means.

158. Remember that the quality of
     your work is a snapshot of
     your character.

159. Live so that when your children think of fairness, caring, and integrity, they think of you.

160. Let your children hear you say things to your wife that lets them know how much you love and treasure her.

Wisdom, compassion, and courage—these are three universally recognized moral qualities of man. When a man understands the nature and use of these moral qualities, he will then understand how to put in order his personal conduct and character.

—CONFUCIUS

161. Measure people by the size of their hearts, not the size of their bank accounts.

162. Never deprive someone of hope. It might be all they have.

163. Remember that love changes everything.

164. Live your life so that your epitaph could read, "No regrets."

165.   Be brave. Even if you're not, pretend to be. No one can tell the difference.

166.   Never compromise your integrity.

167.   Be truthful in all your dealings.

168.   Remember that life's most valuable antiques are dear old friends.

We don't
receive wisdom;
we must discover it
for ourselves after a
journey that no one
can take for us or
spare us.

—MARCEL PROUST

169. Pray not for things, but for wisdom and courage.

170. Never resist a generous impulse.

171. Remember that the direction your life is taking is more important than the speed.

172. Read between the lines.

To be alive,
to be able to see,
to walk, to have a home,
music, paintings, friends—
it's all a miracle. I have
adapted the technique
of living life from
miracle to miracle.

—ARTHUR RUBENSTEIN

*Lessons Learned
That Make Us Wise*

I've learned that most of the things I worry about never happen. —*Age 64*

I've learned that the great challenge of life is to decide what's important and to disregard everything else. —*Age 51*

I've learned that you can't be a hero without taking chances. —*Age 43*

I've learned that a strong code of ethics is as reliable as a compass. —*Age 43*

I've learned that trust is the single most important factor in both personal and professional relationships. —*Age 20*

I've learned that in every face-to-face encounter, regardless of how brief, we leave something behind. —*Age 45*

I've learned that you can do something in an instant that will give you a heartache for life.

—Age 27

I've learned that kindness is more important than perfection.

—Age 70

I've learned that if you look for the worst in life and in people, you'll find it. But if you look for the best, you'll find that instead.

—Age 66

*Wisdom is knowing
what to do next,
skill is knowing
how to do it,
and virtue is
doing it.*

—DAVID S. JORDAN

I've learned that the secret of growing old gracefully is never to lose your enthusiasm for meeting new people and seeing new places. —*Age 75*

I've learned that beyond a certain comfortable style of living, the more material things you have, the less freedom you have. —*Age 62*

I've learned that you shouldn't go through life with a catcher's mitt on both hands. You need to be able to throw something back.

—*Age 66*

I've learned that you must fight for the things you believe in.

—*Age 70*

I've learned that when bad times come, you can let them make you bitter or use them to make you better.

—*Age 75*

I've learned that the simple things are often the most satisfying. —*Age 63*

I've learned that I have never regretted being too generous, but often regretted not being generous enough.

—*Age 76*

I've learned that I don't feel my age as long as I focus on my dreams instead of my regrets. —*Age 83*

I've learned that if you keep doing what you've always done, you'll keep getting what you've always gotten. —*Age 51*

I've learned that I can't change the past, but I can let it go. —*Age 63*

I've learned that a full life is not determined by how long you live, but how well. —*Age 66*

I've learned that the wealthy person is the one who's content with what he has.

—Age 61

I've learned that if you can't forgive and forget, you can at least forgive and move on.

—Age 77

I've learned that there are no unimportant acts of kindness. *—Age 51*

I've learned that deciding who you marry is the most important decision you'll ever make.

—Age 92

I've learned that my greatest fear is that in later years I'll look back at a long list of things I "never got around to."   —*Age 30*

I've learned that an insatiable curiosity is important to never feeling old.   —*Age 71*

I've learned that you can't expect your children to listen to your advice and ignore your example.   —*Age 51*

I've learned that the more a child feels valued, the better his values will be.

—Age 39

I've learned that being too quick to judge someone can deprive you of a great encounter and the possibility of a wonderful long-term relationship. *—Age 40*

I've learned that we are responsible for what we do, no matter how we feel.

—Age 51

To *know how
to grow old is the
master-work of wisdom
and one of the most
difficult chapters in the
great art of living.*

—HENRI F. AMIEL

I've learned that whenever I decide
something with kindness, I usually make
the right decision. —*Age 66*

I've learned that if you want to do
something positive for your children, try
to improve your marriage. —*Age 61*

I've learned that the best advice you can give to anyone is, "Be kind." —*Age 66*

I've learned that it's okay to be content with what you have, but never with what you are. —*Age 51*

I've learned that a person's greatest need is to feel appreciated. —*Age 45*

I've learned that once a woman decides she wants something, never underestimate her ability to get it.

—*Age 34*

I've learned that regardless of how little you have, you can always give comfort and encouragement.

—*Age 64*

I've learned that you should fill your life with experiences, not excuses.   —*Age 51*

I've learned that if you give a pig and a boy everything they want, you'll get a good pig and a bad boy.   —*Age 77*

I've learned that it's better not to wait for a crisis to discover what's important in your life.   —*Age 45*

I've learned that you should treasure your children for what they are, not for what you want them to be.   —*Age 39*

I've learned that a loving, faithful wife is a man's greatest treasure. —*Age 68*

I've learned that life is like a blind date. Sometimes you just have to have a little faith. —*Age 23*

I've learned that my worst decisions were made when I was angry. —*Age 62*

I've learned that bigger is not always better, and that going faster is not necessarily progress. —*Age 73*

I've learned that you can always get more money, but you can never get more time.

—*Age 65*

I've learned that meeting interesting people depends less on where you go than on who you are.

—*Age 51*

I've learned that you never get rewarded for the things you intend to do.

—*Age 76*

Little progress
can be made merely by
attempting to repress what
is evil; our great hope
lies in developing
what is good.

—CALVIN COOLIDGE

I've learned that the trick is to live a long time without growing old. *—Age 73*

I've learned that the best tranquilizer is a clear conscious.

—Age 76

I've learned that when you have a wonderful wife, tell others, but be sure to tell her too. *—Age 51*

I've learned that kind words and good
deeds are eternal. You never know where
their influence will end.

—Age 51

I've learned that old age is not a defeat but
a victory, not a punishment but a
privilege.

—Age 79

I've learned that an act of love, no matter how great or small, is always appreciated.

—*Age 22*

I've learned that no matter how old or how experienced you are, you can always learn something from a child.

—*Age 20*

I've learned that the importance of fame, fortune, and all other things pales in comparison to the importance of positive personal relationships.

—*Age 50*

I've learned that warmth, kindness, and friendship are the most yearned commodities in the world. The person who can provide them will never be lonely.

—Age 79

I've learned that you can sit and worry until you are physically ill, but worrying doesn't change things—action does.

—Age 46

I've learned that maturity has more to do with what types of experiences you've had and what you've learned from them and less to do with how many birthdays you've celebrated.

—*Age 27*

I've learned that children need smiles and hugs more than they need lectures and instructions.

—*Age 48*

I've learned that children follow examples, not advice.

—*Age 62*

I've learned that you shouldn't waste too much of today worrying about yesterday.

—*Age 45*

SUCCESS

1. Remember being nice is always good business.

2. Focus on something that's vital to your business and learn to do it better than anyone else.

3. Type out your five favorite quotations and place them where you can see them every day.

4. Remember the credo of Walt Disney: Think. Believe. Dream. Dare.

5. When you find a job you love, give it everything you've got.

6. Let your word be your bond.

7. Remember that nothing important was ever achieved without someone's taking a chance.

Nobody who
ever gave his best
regretted it.

—George Halas

8. Watch your finances like a hawk.

9. Never work for someone you wouldn't be proud to introduce to your mother.

10. Hold yourself to the same high standards that you require of others.

11. Take advantage of free lectures on any subject in which you are remotely interested.

12. Look for the opportunity that's hidden in every adversity.

13. Remember that the key to your success is determined by what you're willing to sacrifice for it.

14. Never let the odds keep you from pursuing what you know in your heart you were meant to do.

Keep away
from people who
try to belittle
your ambitions.
Small people always
do that, but the really
great make you feel
that you, too, can
become great.

—MARK TWAIN

15. Don't forget that your attitude is just as important as the facts.

16. Try to meet personally with your mayor, city lawmakers, and congressional representatives.

17. Remember that experiences are more valuable than things almost every time.

18. Never regret any money spent on furthering your education.

19. Reread Dale Carnegie's classic, *How To Win Friends and Influence People.*

20. When asking, ask boldly.

The marvelous
richness of human
experience would lose
something of rewarding joy
if there were no limitations
to overcome. The hilltop
hour would not be half so
wonderful if there were
no dark valleys
to traverse.

—HELEN KELLER

21. Remember that the only time you really lose is when you're not giving it 100 percent.

22. Never underestimate your competition.

23. Remember life's problems always seem to look more manageable in the morning.

24. When negotiating price, try to force the other party into making the first offer.

25. Each year read at least three Pulitzer Prize-winning books.

26. Never turn down an opportunity to travel.

27. Even if it's just a line or two, acknowledge in a note any kindness done for you.

Whatever
your hand finds to do, do it with your might.

—ECCLESIASTES 9:10

28. Accept any position in a company that really interests you. Grunt jobs well done often become great jobs.

29. Take advantage of the power of networking. Attend parties and conferences and smile and schmooze no matter how you feel.

30. Don't confuse effort with results.

31. Never drink more than two alcoholic beverages at a social function regardless of how long you're there.

32. Tomorrow ask your boss to name five specific things you can do to help him/her with their job.

Nothing can
stop the man with the
right mental attitude from
achieving his goal;
nothing on earth
can help the man with the
wrong mental attitude.

—THOMAS JEFFERSON

33. Remember the turtle; to get anywhere it has to stick its neck out.

34. Become an expert in an area essential to the success of your company.

35. When you meet people that you admire, ask them the titles of the books they're currently reading.

36. Remember that the quickest way to get a raise is to raise your commitment to the company.

37. Never test the depth of water with both feet.

38. When being firm, always be polite.

39. Read *Undaunted Courage* by Stephen Ambrose.

I*t's no use saying "We are doing our best." You have got to succeed in doing what is necessary.*

—WINSTON CHURCHILL

40. Remember the best antidote for worry is action.

41. Proofread carefully everything that goes out under your signature.

42. When you're not the biggest or fastest, be the one most committed to improvement.

43. To get someone's attention, ask for their opinion.

44. Remember that all people want to be a part of something truly great. We all want to be a member of a winning team.

45. Never sit down to a haircut five minutes before closing.

46. Energize your marriage with appreciation, affection, attention, and acceptance.

Try not to
become a man of
success but rather try
to become a man
of values.

—ALBERT EINSTEIN

47.   This week do what you can to resolve an ongoing conflict you have with someone.

48.   Look for the good. Search for the truth. Hope for the best.

49.   Remember that to be a success, you have to be first, best, or different.

50.   Never assume it's too late to get involved in a good cause.

51. When getting ready for an interview,
     ask yourself the toughest questions
     you're likely to be asked and prepare
     good answers.

52. Volunteer to help, especially when it's
     unexpected.

53. Tell your best friend how much you
     appreciate having him or her in
     your life.

I *want to be thoroughly used up when I die. Life is no brief candle to me; it is a sort of splendid torch which I get ahold of for the moment and I want to make it burn as brightly as possible before handing it on to future generations.*

—GEORGE BERNARD SHAW

54. In your relationships with others, remember that diplomacy is almost always preferable to candor.

55. Never turn back with your head down. Look up, you could be just a few feet from your goal.

56. Pay your bills on time.

57. Remember that a crisis is an opportunity to show the world what you are made of.

58. When interviewing for a job, learn as much as you can about the business by visiting the library and reading the past year's trade magazines covering the industry.

The credit belongs to those who are actually in the arena, who strive valiantly; who know the great enthusiasm, the great devotions, and spend themselves in a worthy cause; who at the best, know the triumph of high achievement; and who, at the worst, if they fail, fail while daring greatly, so that their place shall never be with those cold and timid souls who know neither victory nor defeat.

—THEODORE ROOSEVELT

59. Be flexible with your time but never your values.

❧

60. Remember you'll make fewer mistakes trusting people than not trusting them.

❧

61. Rent the movie *Rudy* and watch it with your family.

❧

62. Never bet against someone who is better prepared and more committed than you.

63. Remember that if you can save money regardless of how limited your income, your success is almost assured.

❧

64. You'll make many mistakes but try to get most of them out of the way by the time you're thirty.

Those who
*turn back never reach
the summit.*

—H. JACKSON BROWN, JR.

65. Live your life as if you were someone's only role model.

66. Never make an important decision after having a couple of drinks or when you're upset.

67. Be constantly looking for ways to help others succeed.

68. Keep your wife's and children's welfare your highest priority.

❧

69. Remember if you're not getting one or two job offers a year, maybe you should be working harder at your present job.

❧

70. Discipline yourself to do the right thing in the right way at the right time.

The first one
gets the oyster,
the second one gets
the shell.

—ANDREW CARNEGIE

71. Make your agenda not one of "getting by," but one of always "getting better."

72. Ask for what you want. Ask again. If you don't get it, what have you lost?

73. Remember that while life doesn't always give us chances, it always gives us choices.

74. Never miss the chance to offer a sincere compliment.

75. Be stronger than your difficulties—braver than your fears—more noble than your temptations.

76. When asked, always express your enthusiasm for your job, your marriage, and your future.

*"I can't do it"
never yet accomplished
anything;
"I will try" has
performed wonders.*

—GEORGE P. BARNHAM

77. Prepare for a successful tomorrow by doing your best today.

78. Never squander money regardless of how much you have.

79. Treat every customer as if he/she is your best customer.

80. Ask yourself, "Where is my job taking me?" Ask yourself, "Where are my relationships taking me?"

81. Even on casual Fridays, don't be too casual.

82. Resist the comfort of conformity.

83. Make waves. Make something happen. Make a difference.

84. Read a biography of someone you've admired.

If we listened to
our intellect, we'd never
have a love affair. We'd
never have a friendship.
We'd never go in business
because we'd be cynical.
Well, that's nonsense.
You've got to jump off
the cliff all the time and
build your wings on
the way down.

—RAY BRADBURY

85. Be five minutes early for appointments.

86. Occasionally when someone asks you a question, respond with, "I don't know; what do you think?" You'll find out what's on their mind.

87. Remember that the speed of the leader is usually the speed of the group.

88. Associate yourself with people who are exemplary in these three areas: intelligence, energy, and integrity.

89. Don't wait until you get your "dream job" before giving it all you've got. Excel at the job at hand and the "dream job" will appear sooner than you thought.

I*t doesn't take talent*
to hustle.

—H. JACKSON BROWN, JR.

90. Never evaluate a person's intellect, talent, or commitment by their appearance.

~

91. Think clearly. Act decisively. Live honorably.

~

92. Remember when hiring that experience is often overrated; passion, character, and creativity are often more important to success.

93. When buying a present for a client, choose the best in its category.

94. Remember that every one of your clients have three invisible words written on their foreheads— Handle with care.

95. Establish goals then aim a little above them.

If things are not
going well with you,
begin your effort of
correcting the situation
by carefully examining the
service you are rendering,
and especially the spirit
in which you are
rendering it.

—Roger Babson

96. Remember that nobody gets to the top without hard work.

97. Do a good job and you won't have to sweat time doing it over, or explaining why you didn't do it right in the first place.

98. When you come up with what you know is a great idea, maintain your passion, commitment, and focus and don't let anybody or anything get in your way.

99. Don't wait for inspiration in order
to begin; begin and inspiration will
find you.

100. Live your life so that you can say
each evening that you have in some
small way contributed to the good
of mankind.

101. Remember that a kick in the behind
usually moves you forward.

Start by doing
what's necessary,
then do what's possible,
and suddenly you are
doing the impossible.

—SAINT FRANCIS OF ASSISI

102. Never forget that every world-changing event or invention was once considered impossible.

103. Make a list of the ten things in your life that matter most. Put it where you can see it every day.

104. Remember that it's the simple things that touch the heart.

105. When you have a gloomy thought, don't share it.

106. Be in the 20 percent of people who can be counted upon to get things done.

107. Life is a dance. Don't sit it out.

…Pray for a task
that will call forth
your faith, your courage,
your perseverance, and
your spirit of sacrifice.
Keep your hands and
your soul clean and the
conquering current
will flow freely.

—THOMAS DREIER

108. Don't worry if your career doesn't immediately take off like a rocket. There are thousands of stories about late bloomers.

109. Never let someone take a photo of you doing something you wouldn't want printed on the front page of your local newspaper.

110. Don't waste time working for a company whose principles don't match your own.

111.   Take a course in leadership.

~

112.   When reading self-help books, include the Bible.

~

113.   Always prepare a Plan B.

When you get
into a tight place and
everything goes against
you, till it seems as though
you cannot hold on a
minute longer,
never give up then,
for that is just the place
and time that the
tide will turn.

—HARRIET BEECHER STOWE

114. Never leave a job interview without telling the interviewer specifically why you should be hired and by offering specific examples of how you can improve the company's business.

115. Remember that satisfaction seldom comes from the things you buy but rather from relationships you nourish and cherish.

116. Promise yourself you won't grow old saying, "I wish I had."

117. Do your homework and be better prepared than anyone else in your group.

118. When attending a conference or study group, introduce yourself to as many people as you can.

No *man*
who is occupied in
doing a very difficult thing,
and doing it very well,
ever loses his
self-respect.

—George Bernard Shaw

119. Remember the more you keep swinging the greater your chance of hitting one out of the park.

120. Don't wait until everything is nearly perfect before being happy or optimistic; be superior to circumstances.

121. Remember that any job done exceptionally well has the potential within it, the seeds of greatness.

122. If you fail, be sure it's a result of dreaming too big, not thinking too small.

123. Take action. All your planning and dreaming is useless unless you do.

We must sail
sometimes with the
wind and sometimes
against it—
but we must sail,
and not drift, nor
lie at anchor.

—OLIVER WENDELL HOLMES

124. Remember that it's never too late to set aside your prejudices.

125. Don't wait until all obstacles are resolved before beginning a new project. If you do, someone else will have seized the opportunity.

126. Try to make everyone you meet feel like they're the most important person you've seen all day.

127. Remember that creativity plus discipline is almost always a formula for success.

128. Judge your success by the degree that you're enjoying peace, health, and love.

129. Never give up on what you really want to do. The person with big dreams is more powerful than one with all the facts.

Proper preparation solves 80 percent of life's problems.

—H. JACKSON BROWN, JR.

130. Take responsibility for every area of your life. Stop blaming others.

❧

131. Choose work that is in harmony with your values.

❧

132. Give your best to your employer. It's one of the best investments you can make.

❧

133. When facing a difficult task, act as though it is impossible to fail.
If you're going after Moby Dick, take along the tartar sauce.

134. Remember that the wisest and most inspired words in the world are merely words unless you apply them to your life.

135. Be bold and courageous. When you look back on your life, you'll regret the things you didn't do more than the ones you did.

I*f I do not
practice one day,
I know it.
If I do not
practice the next,
the orchestra knows it.
If I do not
practice the third day,
the whole world
knows it.*

—IGNACY PADEREWSKI

136.   What you must do, do cheerfully.

137.   Go the distance. When you accept
       a task, finish it.

138.   Take care of your reputation.
       It's your most valuable asset.

139.   Pray. There is immeasurable
       power in it.

140. A racehorse that consistently runs just a second faster than another horse is worth millions of dollars more. Be willing to give that extra effort that separates the winner from the one in second place.

141. Remember if you're prepared, success can come at any time.

Take calculated risks.
This is quite different
from being rash.

—GEORGE S. PATTON

142. Don't live with the brakes on.

143. Never focus on what you are not going to do; focus on what you can do and are going to do.

144. Remember, nothing is a bargain if you don't need it.

145. Watch your attitude. It's the first thing people notice about you.

146. Be the kind of person who brightens a room just by entering it.

147. Smile a lot. It costs nothing and is beyond price.

148. Remember that what you do with what happens to you is more important than what happens to you.

I *have learned that success is to be measured not so much by the position that one has reached in life as by the obstacles which he has overcome while trying to succeed.*

—BOOKER T. WASHINGTON

149. Never forget that it takes only one person or one idea to change your life forever.

150. Commit yourself to a mighty purpose.

Lessons Learned
That Make Us Successful

I've learned that you shouldn't compare yourself to the best others can do, but to the best you can do.   —*Age 68*

I've learned that life challenges us with the fact that everything can be done better.   —*Age 57*

I've learned that you shouldn't call a $100 meeting to solve a $10 problem.   —*Age 55*

I've learned that even the simplest task can be meaningful if I do it in the right spirit.   —*Age 72*

I've learned that if you hire mediocre people, they will hire mediocre people.
                                        —*Age 53*

I've learned that a person's degree of self-confidence greatly determines his success.

—Age 42

I've learned that success is more often the result of hard work than of talent. *—Age 59*

I've learned that if you take good care of your employees, they will take good care of your customers.

—Age 49

I've learned that it's best not to quit at quitting time.

—*Age 37*

I've learned that a good reputation is a person's greatest asset. —*Age 74*

I've learned that it's okay to enjoy your success, but you should never quite believe it. —*Age 63*

Life is
tons of discipline.

—Robert Frost

I've learned that some money costs
too much.

—*Age 51*

I've learned that the person with big
dreams is more powerful than the one
with all the facts. —*Age 51*

I've learned that any activity becomes
creative when you try to do it better than
you did it before. —*Age 48*

I've learned that the best and quickest way to appreciate other people is to try and do their job.   —*Age 51*

I've learned that being a success at the office is not worth it if it means being a failure at home.   —*Age 51*

I've learned that if your life is free of failures, you're probably not taking enough risks.　　　　　—*Age 42*

I've learned that successful living is like playing a violin—it must be practiced daily.　　　　　—*Age 70*

I've learned that when making a decision, no is more easily changed to yes than yes is changed to no. —*Age 55*

I've learned that you can keep going long after you think you can't. —*Age 69*

I've learned that my success stops
when I do.   —*Age 58*

I've learned that if you're the boss and you
stop rowing, you shouldn't be surprised
if everyone else rests too.   —*Age 59*

*Success seems
to be largely a matter
of hanging on after
others have let go.*

—WILLIAM FEATHER

I've learned that everyone can afford to be generous with praise. It's not something available only to the well-to-do.

—*Age 76*

I've learned that what you are thinking about, you are becoming. —*Age 55*

I've learned that there's no elevator to success. You have to take the stairs.

—*Age 48*

I've learned that if you don't focus on the money but on doing a good job, the money will come. —*Age 59*

I've learned that it takes very little extra effort to be considered outstanding.

—*Age 46*

I've learned that going the extra mile puts you miles ahead of your competition.

—*Age 66*

I've learned that making a living is not the same thing as making a life. —*Age 58*

I've learned that if you want to get promoted, you must do things that get noticed. —*Age 54*

I've learned that it is impossible to accomplish anything worthwhile without the help of other people. —*Age 82*

I've learned that the secret of success in business is surprisingly simple: give people more than they expect and do it cheerfully.   —*Age 73*

I've learned that you shouldn't discuss your success with people less successful than you.   —*Age 50*

I've learned that a pat on the back with a sincere "You're doing a great job" can make someone's day.

—*Age 49*

I've learned that no one is ever so powerful or successful that they don't appreciate a sincere compliment.

—*Age 62*

I *never
blame fortune—
there are too many
complicated situations
in life. But, I am
absolutely merciless
toward lack
of effort.*

—F. Scott Fitzgerald

I've learned that you can tell a lot about a man by the happiness of his wife and the respect given him by his children. —*Age 51*

I've learned that enthusiasm and success just seem to go together. —*Age 44*

I've learned that most people resist change, and yet it's the only thing that brings progress. —*Age 66*

I've learned that everybody likes to be asked his or her opinion. —*Age 71*

I've learned that I've never regretted the nice things I've said about people. —*Age 38*

I've learned that people are in such a hurry to get to the "good life" that they often rush right past it. —*Age 72*

I've learned that if you do business with honest people, you must be an honest person.

—*Age 55*

I've learned that if you have several tasks, do the hardest one first, then the rest will be a snap.

—*Age 86*

I've learned that a minute of extra thinking beforehand can save hours of worry later.

—Age 22

I've learned that all the advice and wisdom in the world cannot help you unless you apply it daily in your life.

—Age 23

I've learned that people place too much importance on progress and not enough on maintenance. —*Age 32*

I've learned that you should hope and work, but never hope more than you work. —*Age 59*

I've learned that a peacock today may be a feather duster tomorrow. —*Age 62*

I've learned that a smile is an inexpensive way to improve your looks.   —*Age 17*

I've learned that opportunities are never lost; someone will take one you miss.

—*Age 89*

I've learned that what matters is not that you be the best, but that you try your best.

—*Age 15*

HAPPINESS

1. Whatever you have to do, do it with a cheerful spirit.

2. Remember that happiness comes from virtuous living.

3. When it's not a sunny morning, let your cheerfulness make it one.

4. Remember that laughter is an instant vacation.

5. Learn to make something beautiful with your hands.

6. Remember that a grateful heart is almost always a happy one.

7. Create and maintain a peaceful home.

8. Protect your enthusiasm from negative attitudes of others.

About 90 percent
of the things in our lives
are right and 10 percent
are wrong. If we want to be
happy, all we have to
do is concentrate on the
90 percent and ignore
the 10 percent that
are wrong.

—DALE CARNEGIE

9. On your birthday, send your mom a thank-you card.

10. Keep a scrapbook of your children's accomplishments.

11. Practice random acts of kindness.

12. Start a "smile file" of jokes, articles, and cartoons that make you laugh.

13. Write a poem to your newborn child, present it to her the day she graduates from high school.

14. When you hear something nice said about a friend, tell him so.

15. Save ticket stubs; when rediscovered they will bring back a lot of memories.

*Human felicity
is produced not so
much by great pieces of
good fortune that
seldom happen,
as by little advantages
that occur every day.*

—BENJAMIN FRANKLIN

16. Watch reruns of *The Wonder Years*.

17. Keep fresh flowers on the kitchen table.

18. Visit the Biltmore estate in Asheville, North Carolina, during the spring tulip festival.

19. Surprise someone who's more than eighty years old or a couple celebrating fifty years or more of marriage with a personal greeting from the President. Mail details to The White House, Greetings Office, Room 39, Washington, DC 20500, four to six weeks in advance.

20. Send your mom a Mother's Day corsage.

Make a rule
and pray to God
to help you keep it;
never, if possible, lie down
at night without being able
to say, "I have made one
human being a little wiser
or a little happier or at
least a little better
this day."

—CHARLES KINGSLEY

21. When building a home, make sure to add a screened-in porch.

22. Visit a pet store every once in a while and watch the children watch the animals.

23. Never pass up a chance to be in a parade.

24. Today, tell your dad the one thing he said or did that has meant the most to your happiness and success.

25. Experience Niagara Falls from a boat ride on the *Maid of the Mist.*

26. Don't be discouraged over the opportunities you have missed; there are many more right around the bend.

27. Learn to tie balloons into funny animal shapes.

I *don't know
what your destiny
will be, but one
thing I know:
the only ones among
you who will be really
happy are those who will
have sought and found
how to serve.*

—ALBERT SCHWEITZER

28. Take some silly photos of yourself and a friend in an instant photo booth.

29. Save a snowball from winter in your freezer. Toss it at someone on the Fourth of July.

30. Enter something in the state fair.

31. Send your children lots of mail when they go away to camp or college.

32. Surprise a new neighbor with one of your favorite homemade dishes and include the recipe.

33. Every couple of months, spend thirty minutes or so in a big toy store.

34. Watch *Little Rascals* videos.

M*any persons
have a wrong idea
of what constitutes real
happiness. It is not
obtained through
self-gratification, but
through fidelity to a
worthy purpose.*

—HELEN KELLER

35. Record the birthday heights of your children on the kitchen doorjamb. Never paint it.

36. Go for long, hand-holding walks with your spouse.

37. Kiss slowly. Forgive quickly.

38. When you have a footrace with your kids, let them win at the end.

39. Never run out of crunchy peanut
    butter and vanilla wafers.

40. Wave to train engineers.

41. Take your dad bowling.

42. When baking a cake, let the kids lick
    the beaters.

Getters generally don't get happiness; givers get it. You simply give to others a bit of yourself—a thoughtful act, a helpful idea, a word of appreciation, a lift over a rough spot, a sense of understanding, a timely suggestion. You take something out of your mind, garnished in kindness out of your heart, and put it into the other fellow's mind and heart.

—CHARLES BURR

43. Get up early after a snowfall and shovel your neighbor's walk. If he asks you who did it, say a friend must have.

44. Don't count calories from December 17 through January 2.

45. Never refuse a holiday dessert.

46. On a June evening, pick up some friends and go to a little league baseball game.

47. Always enjoy a gigantic banana split on your birthday.

48. Once in your life be in Times Square on New Year's Eve.

The Constitution
of the United States only
guarantees pursuit of
happiness—you have to
catch up with it yourself.
Fortunately, happiness
is something that depends
not on position, but
disposition, and life is
what you make it.

—GILL ROBB WILSON

49. Take a three to four day road trip by yourself with no destination, no schedule, no reservations, and no particular roads to follow.

50. Take a horse-drawn carriage ride with a loved one through Central Park during a winter snow.

51. Learn to make your grandmother's favorite dessert.

52. Remember that a moment of anger denies you sixty seconds of happiness.

53. Play an April Fools' Day joke on your boss.

54. Every month read a book from the *New York Times* bestsellers list.

There is only
one happiness to life,
to love and be loved.

—GEORGE SAND

55. At least once in your life attend a Jimmy Buffett concert.

56. Watch your children sleeping.

57. Kiss your girlfriend passionately in a crowded elevator.

58. Take off your shoes and socks and enjoy the pleasure of feeling the warmth of where your dog or cat has been lying.

59. Call two friends this week and tell them how much they mean to you.

60. Life is a journey; waltz don't walk.

61. Remember that sometimes the best way to clean a child's room is to just close the door.

62. Own a Louis Armstrong CD with the song "What a Wonderful World" on it.

We act as though comfort and luxury were the chief requirements of life, when all that we need to make us really happy is something to be enthusiastic about.

—CHARLES KINGSLEY

63. Leave your hammock up all year round. When winter comes, wrap yourself up in something warm, go outside, climb in the hammock, and enjoy the first snowfall.

64. Remember that the happiest people are not those getting more, but those giving more.

65. Relearn to play the instrument you started playing in high school.

66. Out of the blue tell your parents you love them, I guarantee they'll smile!

67. If you get the opportunity, dance with a kid.

68. Remember that the more you judge the people in your life, the more unhappy you'll be.

69. If you know someone's on a diet, tell them they're "looking terrific."

Fear less, hope more;
eat less, chew more;
whine less, breathe more;
talk less, say more;
hate less, love more;
and all good things
are yours.

—SWEDISH PROVERB

70. Draw a sketch from memory of your childhood bedroom.

71. When a person compliments your tie, take it off and give it to him. He will never forget the gesture.

72. Show gratitude, if not for what you have now, then for all the good things still ahead.

73. Never forget that contentment is the greatest wealth.

74. Own a CD of The Beach Boys' greatest hits.

75. Reread Truman Capote's short story, "A Christmas Memory" every holiday season.

76. Whisper "I love you" to someone as they are drifting off to sleep.

The time to
be happy is now.
The way to be happy is
to make others so.

—ROBERT INGERSOLL

77. Keep a record of the funny and amazingly clever things your children say.

78. If you still live in the same area, on your wedding anniversary revisit the places you went on your first date.

79. Remember your nephews, nieces, and cousins on their birthdays.

80. At your next meeting with five or ten people, give everyone a box of animal crackers. You'll be delighted with the smiles and comments.

81. This next year try every Baskin-Robbins ice cream flavor.

82. Hide an "I love you madly" note in your sweetie's coat pocket or purse.

*Cherish all your
happy moments;
they make a
fine cushion for
old age.*

—CHRISTOPHER MORLEY

83. Always have pieces of your children's artwork on the fridge.

❧

84. Reread the books you enjoyed reading as a child.

❧

85. Respond by saying, "I am so happy to have had you to give it to," when someone thanks you profusely for a gift or a favor.

86. Send someone you haven't thought about in a long time a card. It will make their day.

87. Remember that it's the simple things that touch the heart.

88. Every once in a while surprise your children by taking them out to breakfast on the way to school.

All you need
for happiness is
a good gun,
a good horse,
and a good wife.

—Daniel Boone

89. Commit time every week to something larger than yourself.

❧

90. Don't waste your time with negative, grumpy people.

❧

91. Every weekend for a year, watch a different Academy Award-winning movie.

❧

92. Never forget that regardless of where you are on life's journey, something unexpected and amazing can lie just around the bend.

93. Keep your mind open to new possibilities.

94. Remember that it's life's little detours that often offer the best scenery.

95. Remember that you never lose when you sacrifice for those things bigger than yourself.

Happiness can be
built only on virtue,
and must of necessity
have truth for its
foundation.

—SAMUEL TAYLOR COLERIDGE

96. The next time you pick up a friend or relative at the airport, park the car, buy a couple of balloons or a bouquet of flowers, and meet them at the gate. They will never forget it.

97. Remember that when it really comes down to it, few things are worth getting upset about.

98. Save the favorite Christmas cards you received and look at them again on July 4.

❧

99. Give plenty of hugs. You never know how long it's been since they've received the last one.

❧

100. Let your children be children. They only have ten to fifteen years to be young and innocent and about sixty years to be mature, serious adults.

If one only wished
to be happy, this would be
easily accomplished;
but we wish to be happier
than other people,
and this is always difficult,
for we believe others
to be happier than
they are.

—CHARLES DE SECONDAT MONTESQUIEU

101. Forgive quickly and don't hesitate to ask others to forgive you.

102. Always compliment the cook.

103. Remember that finding just the right gift for someone is almost as wonderful as getting a gift yourself.

104. Refrain from trying to straighten out everyone's problems.

105. Remember that success is not the key to happiness—happiness is the key to success.

106. Offer several hours of your time every month to a group or organization that helps those in need and for which your only compensation is the joy of doing it.

The foolish man
seeks happiness in
the distance;
the wise grows it
under his feet.

—JAMES OPPENHEIM

107. Regardless of our talents, remember that we all have the gift to be a good friend.

108. Learn to recognize and enjoy life's simple pleasures—there are so many of them.

109. Don't be surprised at the increased happiness that results from even small courtesies given and received.

110. When you arrive at your job in the morning, let the first thing you say brighten someone's day.

111. Refrain from envy. It's the source of much unhappiness.

112. Your mind can only hold one thought at a time. Make it a positive and constructive one.

113. Don't postpone joy.

To *be happy*
is not the purpose
of our being,
but to deserve
happiness.

—IMMANUEL H. FICHTE

Lessons Learned That Make Us Happy

I've learned that it's better to be married to someone with a good nature than a good physique.   —*Age 39*

I've learned that if you pursue happiness, it will elude you. But if you focus on your family, the needs of others, your work, meeting new people, and doing the very best you can, happiness will find you.

—*Age 65*

I've learned that nothing is more fun than a job you enjoy.   —*Age 29*

I've learned that more comfort doesn't necessarily mean more happiness. —*Age 55*

I've learned that brushing my child's hair is one of life's greatest pleasures.   —*Age 29*

I've learned that the best way to cheer up yourself is to cheer up someone else.

—*Age 13*

I've learned that there are two things essential to a happy marriage—separate checking accounts and separate bathrooms.

—*Age 36*

I've learned that happiness is like perfume: you can't give it away without getting a little on yourself.

—*Age 59*

I've learned that I have never been bored in the presence of a cheerful person.

—*Age 63*

I've learned that you know your husband still loves you when there are two brownies left and he takes the smaller one.

—*Age 39*

I've learned that for a happy day, look for something bright and beautiful in nature. Listen for a beautiful sound, speak a kind word to some person, and do something nice for someone without their knowledge.

—Age 85

I've learned that my best friend and I can do anything or nothing and have the best time.

—Age 18

I've learned that the easiest way to find happiness is to quit complaining. —*Age 19*

I've learned that a mother is only as happy as her child. —*Age 49*

I've learned that a happy journey almost always depends on choosing the right traveling companions. —*Age 65*

I've learned that an afternoon in my garden is better than an afternoon with a therapist. —*Age 37*

I've learned that there's nothing sweeter than sleeping with your babies and feeling their breath on your cheeks. —*Age 38*

I've learned that people love to get letters from friends and family, no matter what the subject is or the length of the letters.

—*Age 22*

I've learned that I like to plant my neighbors' favorite flowers in my flower boxes so that they can see and enjoy them.

—*Age 50*

I've learned that it's fun to brighten someone's day by surprising her with a plate of homemade chocolate chip cookies.

—*Age 20*

I've learned that when I feel down, nothing picks me up like hearing my mom say, "I'm proud of you."

—*Age 22*

I've learned that the size of a house has nothing to do with how happy it is inside.

—Age 22

I've learned that the thing that gives me the most joy is writing to my eighty-three-year-old sister.

—Age 86

I've learned that when I can't sleep in the middle of the night, I find great joy in watching my husband and children sleeping peacefully.

—Age 37

I've learned that simple walks with my father around the block on summer nights when I was a child did wonders for me as an adult.

—Age 18

I've learned that no matter how serious your life requires you to be, everyone needs a friend to act goofy with.

—Age 21

I've learned that if you are happy, it is because you put others before yourself.

—*Age 86*

I've learned that if you share your garden, you will be rewarded tenfold.   —*Age 44*

I've learned that there's nothing better on a rainy day than soup, television, and a nap on the couch.   —*Age 21*

I've learned that nothing beats a hot summer night, a car full of friends, the windows down, music playing, and whistling at boys! —*Age 18*

I've learned that there is nothing like the feel of warm mud between your toes.

—*Age 22*

I've learned that just one person saying to me, "You've made my day!" makes my day.

—*Age 20*

I've learned that when I mentally list all the little joys the day has brought me before I fall asleep, I rarely have a sleepless night.

—*Age 44*

I've learned that there is a great thrill in making pickles and jellies with the same friend I used to make mud pies with.

—*Age 60*

I've learned that when you are really stressed out, the cure is to put two miniature marshmallows up your nose and try to "snort" them out.   —*Age 11*

I've learned that it's all worth it when you are doing a sink full of dishes and your eighteen-year-old comes up behind you and gives you a big hug. And you ask, "What was that for?" And she replies, "No special reason." —*Age 42*

I've learned that even with the lights out, I can still find the cashews in the mixed nuts. —*Age 50*

I've learned that there is nothing better than to sit in the straw and hold a new foal's head in my lap. —*Age 15*

I've learned that happiness is not how much you have but your capacity to enjoy what you have. —*Age 44*

I've learned that if you want an immediate high, give a homeless person ten dollars. —*Age 32*

I've learned that there is no feeling quite so nice as your child's hand in yours.

—*Age 37*

I've learned that bragging on your children is one of life's greatest pleasures.

—*Age 32*

I've learned that the more content I am with myself, the fewer material things I need. —*Age 36*

I've learned that no one was put here to be in charge of making me happy. That's my job.
　　　　　　　　　　　　　　　—Age 42

I've learned that you never outgrow the enjoyment of browsing in the toy department.
　　　　　　　　　　　　　　　—Age 61

I've learned that the best therapy in the world is driving my convertible on a sunny day with no destination in mind.
　　　　　　　　　　　　　　　—Age 25

I've learned that nothing is quite as good as the first scoop of peanut butter out of a new jar. —*Age 34*

I've learned that you can make anyone smile if you give them a box of crayons and a coloring book. —*Age 21*

I've learned that it's not what you have in your life but who you have in your life that counts. —*Age 30*

I've learned that giving flowers makes me just as happy as receiving them. —*Age 23*

I've learned that whoever said you can't buy happiness forgot about puppies.

—*Age 28*

Happiness is…

unexpected courtesies.

anything made of cashmere.

the fragrance of Safari perfume
on my sweet wife's neck.

rooting for the home team.

Happiness is…

donating a pint of blood.

saying "I love you" and hearing
the reply "I love you, too."

the song "The Prayer" sung by
Celine Dion and Andrea Bocelli.

Happiness is...

the feeling of reverence when
you enter a sacred place.

a bold creative thought.

an upgrade to first class on a
long flight because your boss
thinks you deserve it.

Happiness is...

smiling at a little kid and getting
a big smile in return.

anniversary rides in a limo.

never running out of hot water.

discovering something you've always
wanted on sale half price.

Happiness is...

perfectly ripe homegrown tomatoes.

the movie *Father of the Bride*.

warm homemade brownies and
a tall glass of cold milk.

cheerful attitudes.

Happiness is…

my eight-year-old reaching for my hand
when we walk down the street.

a "thinking of you" note from a friend.

mailing a college student a
funny greeting card.

the enthusiastic way my
golden retriever greets me when
I arrive home from work.

Happiness is...

a neighbor's friendly wave.

freshly squeezed grapefruit juice.

homemade soup simmering on the stove.

leaving a quarter in the pay phone
for the next person to find.

Happiness is…

paying someone a compliment.

Junior Mints.

naps on Sunday afternoons.

using your jumper cables to start
a stranger's dead battery.

Happiness is…

animal crackers shared with a child.

little marshmallows in a cup
of hot chocolate.

a perfect dental check-up.

resisting temptation.

Happiness is…

clean, crisp sheets.

photos of you and your friends made
in an instant photo booth.

feeling great after a serious illness.

humility.

Happiness is...

a loved one falling asleep in your arms.

a child's goodnight prayer.

screened-in porches.

grammar school Christmas pageants.

Happiness is...

waking up to winter's first snowfall.

slow dancing cheek-to-cheek.

the smell of new-mown grass.

standing and singing
the national anthem while holding
your hand over your heart.

Happiness is…

tomato soup and a grilled
cheese sandwich.

underwear still warm from the dryer.

an early morning walk on the beach.

a postcard from a friend far away.

Happiness is…

second honeymoons.

repairmen who arrive on time.

the smell of Johnson's Baby Powder.

Truman Capote's "A Christmas Memory."

Happiness is...

a favorite pair of jeans.

overtipping an exceptionally
attentive waitress.

campfire sing-alongs.

a hotel room nicer than you imagined.

Happiness is...

4-H club exhibits at county fairs.

braiding your daughter's hair.

second-hand bookstores.

a hand to hold when life gets slippery.

Happiness is…

anything a kid gives you that
they made at camp.

dual control electric blankets.

indulging yourself after completing
a difficult task.

cheeseburgers.

Happiness is…

hot oatmeal sweetened with
real maple syrup.

browsing through an old
hardware store.

the first day of the year warm
enough to wear shorts.

loyal friends.

Happiness is...

giving a big smile to the greeter
at Wal-Mart.

awakening to the aroma of coffee
brewing and bacon frying.

my child running to me with
outstretched arms.

looking back with few regrets.

Other books by H. Jackson Brown, Jr.

The Complete Life's Little Instruction Book
A Father's Book of Wisdom
P.S. I Love You
Life's Little Instruction Book™
    (volumes I, II, and III)
Live and Learn and Pass It On
    (volumes I, II, and III)
Wit and Wisdom from the Peanut Butter Gang
The Little Book of Christmas Joys
    (with Rosemary C. Brown and Kathy Peel)
A Hero in Every Heart (with Robyn Spizman)
Kids' Little Treasure Books
    On Happy Families
    On What We've Learned . . . So Far
Life's Little Treasure Books
    On Marriage and Family, On Wisdom,
    On Joy, On Success, On Love,
    On Parenting, Of Christmas Memories,
    Of Christmas Traditions, On Hope,
    On Friendship, On Fathers, On Mothers,
    On Things That Really Matter,
    On Simple Pleasures
Life's Little Instruction Book™ *for Incurable*
    Romantics (with Robyn Spizman)
Life's Little Instruction Book™ *from Mothers*
    to Daughters (with Kim Shea)
Life's Little Instructions from the Bible
    (with Rosemary C. Brown)
A Book of Love for My Son
    (with Hy Brett)
A Book of Love for My Daughter
    (with Kim Shea and Paula Y. Flautt)
Highlighted in Yellow
    (with Rochelle Pennington)